**BEYOND BLACK
THERE IS NO COLOUR**

*This is a work of imaginative fiction,
inspired by the life of Iranian poet Forough Farrokhzad.*

Part One

The traffic is dense in downtown Tehran. My taxi driver drops me off a few blocks from my destination and I walk through the Lalehzar Quarter, past shopkeepers chatting while drinking tea from tiny glass cups and trying to lure customers into their boutiques with toothy smiles. I am wearing big sunglasses and an old dress that once belonged to my sister Pouran. It is made of light blue cotton with buttons from top-to-toe and it swishes breezily against my ankles as I walk. It usually gives me a sense of protection because it belonged to my beloved and closest sibling, but today it feels too warm and seems to be clinging to my skin. Midday heat lingers in the polluted streets. It is difficult to breathe properly.

I pause at one of my favourite shops in the world. Notebooks and pens are displayed in the window, just as they were at the beginning of each school term of my childhood. If I enter to buy just one pen I might be in the shop all day. Pens have characters; even two seemingly identical nibs incline me to write differently, so choosing is a difficult task. At the sight of all the notebooks lined up in the window I feel the same flurry of anticipation for clean pages, fresh ink, and new beginnings. If only I could crack myself open like a new notebook, and know that there were hundreds of blank pages waiting to be filled. It is tempting to continue buying notebooks just for the challenge of filling them. Each pen and piece of paper has its own character even though they might look identical at first sight. Each pen writes differently when it comes into contact with different textures of paper. I am twenty-one years old and yet have already been through too many notebooks: wife at sixteen, mother at seventeen, divorcee at nineteen. I published my first poetry collection at twenty, and had a nervous breakdown a few months after. Now I hope to start a new page, in Europe, and am on my way to pick up a visa from the UK embassy.

Ferdowsi Avenue is hot and crowded, with sticky pollution kicking up around my feet. I am going to be late if I don't speed up but as I turn towards the embassy I suddenly feel as if the air is much too thick for my lungs. I pause, then my eyes catch up with my instincts and I see my ex-husband walking down the opposite side of the road. Parviz is formally dressed in a beige summer suit with a light shirt and a tie that doesn't match the rest of his outfit. His hair looks much greyer than the last time we met, or maybe the brightness of the sun is creating a silver shine over him. I haven't seen him since moving away from our house in Ahvaz and back to Tehran.

At the sight of Parviz, feelings of desperation invade my body and the palms of my hands sweat with fear. He is walking a little in front of me, winding through pedestrians on the opposite side of the busy road. I strain to keep him in sight, walking fast now and bumping into people. Parviz makes his way out of Ferdowsi Avenue and towards the statue of the tenth-century poet after whom the road is named. I follow a little way behind, forgetting my appointment now. Parviz stops under the statue, and I have a moment to catch my breath while he searches for something in his bag. He wipes sweat from his brow and I lean on a cold stone wall, trying to steady myself. This is a man I once loved desperately and perhaps still do. A man I made a family with. A man who I believe doesn't respect me. A man who tells my son I abandoned him.

One of the stories from Ferdowsi's national epic, *Shahnameh* ('Book of Kings'), comes into my head while I watch Parviz. In *Shahnameh* an almighty hero named Rostam conceives a son one night and the child is brought up by his mother without Rostam's help. The boy grows up to be a great fighter named Sohrab who wants to prove that he is the strongest man in the country by fighting his own father. The epic story reaches its apogee in the second part of the book when the father kills Sohrab while unaware that this opponent is his son. As the country's second strongest man lies dying in the battlefield, Rostam realises the identity of his brilliant opponent. Although it is a devastating moment, the poem praises Rostam for remaining faithful to his reputation and proving himself an invincible hero. In the end the dying son is proudly recognised as the son of mighty Rostam, and the woman who raised him is hardly mentioned. It seems to me that in the last ten centuries not much has changed; men are accepted and admired in their paternal roles without effort.

My sin was to pursue a career as a poet and to desire an identity beyond that of wife and mother. As a result, I am not worthy of being a significant part of my son's life anymore. I was written off for daring to believe I could exist as an individual rather than simply an extension of my family. Although it is standard for fathers to be given custody of children in divorce cases in Iran, I never imagined that Parviz would cut me off completely.

I have sent my son so many letters and he has not been allowed to answer a single one.

I always hoped that Parviz would accept me as a lover and poet as well as wife and mother. He seemed capable of this when we first met, but then listened to conservative opinions and let rumours destroy his confidence in me, putting an end to our love story. A crowd moves in front of the poet's statue and I realise I have lost Parviz from my sight. I walk forward, pushing through shoppers and businessman, trying to catch him again. My heart beats fast and I see that he is walking straight towards me across the road, getting closer with each adamant step. I turn to walk away. I do not feel brave enough to speak with him.

'Stop rushing off, Forough,' he says loudly. 'Are you really in such a hurry?'

I am struck dumb; yet again he has gained the upper hand. He is the pursuer, the hunter, and I the passive victim. I feel sixteen again, like I am waiting for him to pick me up from the school gates. As he approaches me I see how tense the muscles of his face are, and the macho way he is walking makes me shiver. He was brought up as a prince in the eyes of his adoring parents and when I left it hurt his pride badly. The sun pounds down on me and I feel incapable of speech or movement.

When I don't immediately respond he smirks slightly and says, even louder: 'Don't pretend you can't hear me. Do you want to see your son again?'

I open my mouth to say yes, but before I can speak he interrupts:

'Then fuck me here in the street in front of everyone, and maybe I'll let you.'

He pauses, as if waiting for an answer, then turns and walks away with a look of disgust on his face. Everyone in the busy street stares at me. Some people stop. I want to disappear beneath the surface of the earth and never come back. This is the most humiliating moment of my life; more humiliating than being whipped by my father.

My soul bleeds and the crowds sway on the pavement around me. I start to tremble, as if an ice-cold wind had broken through the city heat. Maybe I will stay frozen here forever. I can't see any distinct shapes, just a cloud of movement. I can't hear the traffic, just a ringing in my ears. I don't know how long I stand there before a voice appears as if from the bottom of a well. '*Khanoom, khanoom*' (Miss? Miss?) the voice says.

I start to run towards the middle of the street and wave down a taxi. There are passengers in the back so I jump in the front and sit there, speechless, while the taxi moves through the streets. The driver doesn't say a word, and nor do the other passengers. I am diminished to dust.

A few years were enough to change our love from one extreme to another. Was that inhuman monster on Ferdowsi Avenue the same person who promised to love and protect me?

Once I asked him: 'Promise me to be always in the same colour.'

'What do you mean?' he said.

'I mean, please stay the same way, the colour of the skies.'

'I will,' he said.

I had naively thought that marriage would be a path to freedom. My father was a colonel in the army and ruled our family as if we were his soldiers. He had a high position in the Cossack Brigade of Reza Khan and during my early childhood his job involved supervising construction in the province of Mazandaran. It was well known that the majority of his construction workers were scared of him, and that he advocated use of the whip to make them work harder. My father seemed to have no more empathy for his family. We were woken early every morning to do military-style exercises on the patio, regardless of snow or searing heat. He whipped us any time we had the audacity to disobey or displease him and since I was born believing that rules were there to be broken, I was punished regularly. I had an urge to mark myself as different, and to say exactly what was on my mind. I constantly wanted to show my father that I was an individual with thoughts and feelings, rather than just a soldier following his orders.

My mother tried to protect us but she was a slave to her husband and children, locked in a perpetual cycle of housework. She was a physically little person and the strain of giving birth to and looking after seven children was visible in deep furrows of pain on her face. She always looked tired and resigned. When I think of her, the image I see is one of her doing some tedious domestic chore. She hardly had any time to herself and didn't insist on creating it. She never dared to complain and always kept her feelings to herself. She showed all her children unconditional love, but she rarely stood up for us against our father. I wondered if she knew how horrible it was to be part of such an inflexible family structure. Perhaps she couldn't see beyond his authoritarian rules. To me, their relationship seemed sad and one-sided.

Before I was born, our family moved from Mazandaran province in the north of Iran to a house at the end of a narrow and dark alley in Tehran. Then we moved again, this time to Amiriyeh, a district in central Tehran. Most of my childhood memories are from this house in Amiriyeh. It was two stories high and surrounded by such high walls that hardly any light seemed to get into the rooms or the garden. It had a pond with frogs in it, and a stream lined with Acacia trees. In the garden there were fig and sour cherry trees. In the years before starting school, I spent most of my time playing with my siblings or the neighbourhood children in this garden. I enjoyed climbing the trees and the walls, howling from the top like an animal or gliding my arms like an airplane. All the neighbourhood children would get together in the small streets and I took pleasure in fighting with the boys, proving that my courage matched theirs. I never saw myself as weaker because I was a girl. I would hit and bite and pull the kids' hair. In some ways, being nothing but an inconsequential daughter in my father's eyes meant that he often didn't notice where I was. On the other hand, flaunting was in my nature. I have always loved the forbidden. I have always desired to be fearless.

Despite the beatings and the lack of recognition, I do owe my father a great deal. He attached great importance to education and inspired my love of literature. He was a passionate book collector and we all learned to read before we started school. Even by banning me from reading certain books, he fuelled my curiosity and desire to learn. My older sister Pouran and I would spend hours locked in the bathroom or hiding in trees devouring books he had forbidden us to touch, even though we were punished whenever he discovered this disobedience. Pouran was my best friend and confidant. She had a calm personality and a way of doing as she pleased without getting in trouble. We read Ferdowsi's *The Book of Kings* for the first time tucked away in that bathroom. The thirst to learn was unstoppable. I loved escaping from the dreary claustrophobia of reality, into a world of adventure and imagination.

I have many fond memories from my childhood. I was the third child. My closest confident was Pouran, but I also adored my younger brother Ferydoun. He was a creative and sensitive boy. I had a difficult relationship with my older brother, who resembled my father in his desire for order and discipline above all else. Pouran, Ferydoun and I particularly loved listening to my grandfather's stories. My grandfather was a talented storyteller and would embellish and stretch even the most banal tales into something magical, teaching us new depths of melancholy and joy. This is when my love for writing started.

Pouran and I would spend hours playing in our courtyard with its little stream passing through the middle. We loved dangling our feet in the water so the goldfish had to find pathways around our toes. The roof of the house was flat so on summer evenings my eldest brother Amir would sweep it and bring the beds and mosquito nets out. Pouran and I shared a bed with a single *lahaf* (quilt) and pillow so we could stay up for hours telling each other stories. Poor mother always had to tell us off several times before we went to sleep.

Our family was full of surprises. When my mother was pregnant with her seventh child, my father gathered us all around him in the main living room to make an important announcement. We sat down nervously, some of us kneeling on the floor, and he cleared his throat in preparation for what he was going to say. He tended to use the minimum of words to the maximum effect. That day was no different.

'I am taking another wife and starting another family,' he said.

Silence fell in the room and we all became like lifeless statues. As a confident dictator, he had not spared a thought to softening the blow of this revelation. I remember staring at my mother's frozen, devastated face. I wondered if she had even been told in advance. Nobody moved or spoke for an age but I felt outrage bubbling in my throat and eventually selfish words came flying out of my mouth:

'Oh Baba,' I said. 'What about me? I wanted to study!'

He cast me an icy stare. I assumed that once he married again, he would forget about us and there would be no money for my education.

'You have learned quite enough already.'

His abandonment was blunt and loveless. My thirteen-year-old brother Ferydoun began to cry. 'Baba,' my brother said while tears fell down his face.

'Ferydoun, you should be ashamed of yourself, crying like a child,' our father said. 'A son doesn't cry.'

I was born into a country that was being dramatically modernised and Westernised. Secular schools were introduced under the reign of Reza Shah. Head scarves and veils were banned along with any visible sign of religious belief. Young people were approached on the streets if they were adhering to the Islamic dress code, and sent home to change. But this desire to eliminate the influence of the Shia clergy met with opposition and the first instances of Islamic extremism began to appear. As a colonel in Reza Khan's Cossack Brigade my father was at the forefront of these changes. Pouran and I were the first to attend a coeducational primary school in our neighbourhood. Our part of town was a typical middle-class area and we belonged to the new urban middle class who were expected to have modern values. Yet the day-to-day life in our neighbourhood was hardly different from other, older parts of the city, filled with little shops offering fresh bread, fruit, vegetables, meat, sweets and household items. The bazaar was not far away and it always felt busy.

The general climate of Iran changed when Reza Shah was deposed in 1941. I was seven years old. Under Allied occupation now, the country was entirely in the hands of foreign powers. This is when a nationalistic fervour began brewing, and a desire to return to more traditional values in order to resist the influence of the Russian and British troops. Of course, I was too young to understand the nuances of these changes, but I knew that we were now to be sent to an all-girls secondary school called Khosrow Khavar High School (ironically, it was named after a man). By the time I finished the ninth grade, xenophobia was widespread and the search for national and traditional values was becoming fevered.

I found refuge in poetry from a young age and I grew up fast. I was writing poems at six or seven, but would tear them into tiny pieces so my father would never find them. Although it was my father who had awakened my love of words and literature through his book collection, he never approved of me being a poet. I was writing regular verses by thirteen and at age fifteen I began attending a school where I was taught to draw, paint and sew. I had a strong passion for the arts and expressing myself both through debate and creativity. Often after class I would meet my friend Sohrab Sepehri, who later became one of Iran's most important contemporary painters. We would go to one of our houses, or sit by the side of the street, reading out loud to each other from poems we had composed.

The preparations for Norouz, Iranian New Year's Day, would start weeks in advance. The day falls on the vernal equinox and marks the beginning of spring in the Northern Hemisphere. It is a day to celebrate rebirth and renewal, a tradition from Zoroastrianism, the pre-Islamic religion from which many of our customs are derived.

Just as nature renews its leaves in spring, it is traditional to wear new clothes for Norouz. One year my mother and I put together the most beautiful outfit for the day: a red polka dot dress, fresh white knee-high socks and shiny black leather shoes. A few days before Norouz some friends came round after school and I couldn't resist showing off my outfit to them. I paraded around my bedroom, making everyone laugh, until I heard the creak of my door opening and saw my mother standing there. She was livid and I'd never seen her so upset with me before. She ordered my friends to go home and then she slapped me several times around the face. As the palms of her hands made contact with my skin, I had mixed feelings about what I had done. Although sad to disappoint her, this guilt was mixed with something electric, and bright. I later had a similar feeling of tugging guilt and profound excitement when I published a controversial poem.

That night Pouran and I chatted and laughed in bed. I felt a sense of satisfaction at not obeying the house rules.

I loved to steal the fistful of keys our mother kept in a kitchen drawer and lead missions around the house finding out what key opens what door. I was insatiably curious and could never resist the allure of a locked door. I loved trespassing.

There are a few moments in my life that stand out as pivotal. My sister's wedding was one of these. To me marriage seemed a door to adulthood, and I was frustrated not to have the key. On her wedding day I was sixteen years old, and she was eighteen. Our knowledge about love and sex came mostly from magazines but we both knew we wanted to leave the close supervision of our parents, to wear bright red lipstick and black eyeliner, to pluck our eyebrows and do what we pleased. This strong desire to grow older faster was a driving force within me and it accelerated the pace with which I ran towards marriage.

From the moment Pouran decided to get married, everything changed. I was going to lose my partner in crime, the person who I could climb into bed with and talk to about my feelings or ambitions. She was the only person in the world who truly understood me and I had infinite respect for the pragmatic way she dealt with our father. She believed that he would never be proud of his daughters, so we should simply not waste any time pursuing praise from him. She placated him, dodged him, pretended to agree with him, but never sought his approval. I envied this logic because despite how cruel my father could be, I desperately wanted his approval. I just wanted him to engage me in an intellectual conversation or take me seriously for one minute, but he was not ready to accept that a woman had the capacity for intelligent conversation. His mind had been shaped by the social parameters of our society.

Pouran's wedding was full of excitement. From first thing in the morning, family and friends brought over flowers and sweets as if our house was the centre of the world. Wedding ceremonies usually take place in an intimate room of the bride's house, so only family and close friends attend. I was allowed to take the whole day off school to help set up the *Sofreh Aghd*, or traditional wedding ceremony spread. I painted eggs with gold paint as a symbol of fertility, and arranged sweets in bowls.

The centre of the *Sofreh Aghd* is always a mirror, a symbol of clarity. The first time the couple see each other during the ceremony is when the bride removes her veil and meets the groom's eyes in the reflection. Two candelabras are placed on either side of the mirror, made of silver and gold, symbolising the warmth and brightness of the couple's future together. Fire and light are important elements of Zoroastrianism.

At every step of the ceremony I imagined myself in my sister's place. As her veil lifted to reveal her face I imagined it was my face, as sugar cones were rubbed above her head to pour happiness down on her, I imagined it was my happiness.

The scent of rosewater *Gholab*, made with roses of Isfahan, was so strong that I could hardly smell the *Esfand* incense that was burnt to keep bad spirits away. Tears of happiness rolled down my mother's face while my father's face was strong and proud.

During the ceremony, my attention was repeatedly drawn to a man I didn't recognise. He was older than me with tanned skin and an intelligent face. He wore a dark grey suit over his slim body, his long hair pulled back at the nape of his neck. To my memory our paths had never crossed until the wedding.

After the bride and groom had exchanged a finger dipped in honey, we all moved into a larger room in the house and the man from the ceremony immediately smiled at me and made me blush. He made his way closer to where I was talking quietly to one of my siblings. Before he even spoke I felt my face burning red as fire. I didn't even dare to look into his eyes but was immediately attracted to him. Oh how I wished to be older and wiser. I would have given anything for a little experience in the art of seduction.

'How are you, Forough?' he asked.

I was unable to utter even one word in reply, wondering how he knew my name. I slowly lifted my head and silently met his tender gaze. Tears filled my eyes, but he was gallant enough not to mention this. I had no idea what it meant to fall in love, but knew that my life would never be the same again.

There are walls everywhere. One wall separates our houses, one separates our gardens and finally one more separating our hearts.

After the wedding we wrote each other letters constantly, and my brother Ferydoun delivered them secretly. His name was Parviz and he was a neighbour and distant cousin who my sister told me worked at Iran's Finance Ministry in Ahvaz but was also a cartoonist and satirist whose stories and sketches had been published in numerous magazines. He occasionally found ways to meet me, usually on my walk to or back from school. One day it was snowing and he waited on the pavement for me, then walked me to school. I was an open book to him and deeply in love from the very start. If I said half a sentence he would know the rest. This frightened me but at the same time it felt like protection. He knew how I felt, how I thought, and he still wanted to be near me. It felt as if I was being taken seriously for the first time in my life and I soon began to trust him. As our letters continued and our love deepened, we began discussing marriage. I knew that my father would be set against it. Parviz was much older than me, but more significantly, he was not a wealthy man. However, I was sure this man was the love of my life and we would be married eventually.

Persuading my parents was a bumpy road. I broached the subject first with my mother, who showed a great deal of understanding and promised that she would try to find an appropriate time to discuss it with my father. Parviz then wrote to him asking for my hand in marriage, and my mother passed the letter on with a positive introduction. All did not go well, however. He didn't think that a civil servant would be able to support me financially and so Parviz was given an impossible list of financial expectations. My father demanded written confirmation that Parviz had access to a considerable sum of money, which he knew Parviz would never be able to provide.

On our walk to school after Parviz had asked for my hand in marriage, we were both gloomy.

'He is stubborn and dislikes revisiting decisions,' I told Parviz.

'Give me some time to find the best way, and trust me,' Parviz said with confidence. It was energising to feel this certainty from his side.

In the end he took out a loan from a local bank in order to show my father he had funds. My parents finally agreed, but told me that no money would be invested in the wedding. I wore the same dress as Pouran, used the same decorations and candle holders. We had fewer guests, and my father's face did not look on with pride. The message was clear: disapproval rather than celebration. But I was happy.

Again, the walls. The walls surround everything. They separate, hide, block the noise of screams and cries. They protect secrets.

Once married, I moved into my husband's family house. They lived in Ahvaz, the capital of Khuzestan Province in the southwest of Iran. Ahvaz is one of the hottest cities on the planet – during summer months it regularly reaches a stifling forty-five degrees. This was a dry and sweaty desert heat that clouded the mind and intensified the emotions. Sandstorms and dust storms regularly swept through sending the population scurrying indoors.

When Parviz and I were alone together life was wonderful. He seemed open-minded, and we had fun together. We spent hours discussing our favourite books and poems while relaxing in his parents' garden or walking together by the river. Until marriage, our relationship had developed in snatched moments and clandestine letters, so it was thrilling to luxuriate in each other's company and discover all the nuances of his personality. I was so excited by the prospect of beginning our lives together.

However, he had to work extremely hard to support us and was often away for weeks at a time. I would be left with his parents in a city where I had no friends, and a rhythm of loneliness began to creep in. His mother did not approve of me at all, and rarely tried to hide her feelings. From the start she was critical of my literary ambitions, my clothes and my demeanour. She showed no respect for my work and would often tell Parviz how much she disapproved of me being a poet. She believed that a woman should take care of the household, cook for her husband and give up all her personal ambitions and self-expression.

To me it did not seem unreasonable that when Parviz was away I would travel back to Tehran to see my own family and meet with people from literary magazines. Those early days of marriage were a time of great inspiration, perhaps due to the heady mixture of love, loneliness and freedom. I wrote poetry regularly and magazines began to publish them, quickly gaining me a certain acclaim in literary circles.

One of the first and most divisive was a poem that described an erotic encounter from the female perspective. It caused a huge uproar both in literary circles and in my home life. After the publication malicious rumours immediately began to spread about me. How could a woman dare to write about love, when until now this was a subject reserved for men? How could a woman dare write about her body, when until now this was a subject reserved for men? Who were the subjects of my poetry? Were they about my husband, or about other men? Up until this point Parviz had been supportive of my poetry, but when this poem was published he began to listen to gossip. I tried to persuade him that I was innocent and the poem was about him. He claimed to believe me, but no longer wanted me to travel when he was away.

My poems spoke the truth – they were how I lived – whereas other poets tried to apply the morals set by society and religion. Other poets desired to compose erudite poems, but why is it that nobody wanted to compose sincere poems? I saw new possibilities for Persian poetry, walking the road paved by the father of modern poetry Nima Yushij. I did not give up. I would not let others tell me how to live. As my poetry continued to be published, critics from all over the country started to send letters to the publisher and complain about my work. The clergy from Qom openly attacked the publication of such poems, as did the narrow-minded bourgeoisie. They liked pretending to be saints themselves while arguing that a poem could corrupt society. They were all hiding behind masks and never wanted to admit the truth.

When we realised I was pregnant, Parviz became even more critical of my travels and my poetry. It was as if the views of his highly traditional mother were gradually being transferred to him. Now that I was to be a mother, apparently I could not simultaneously be a poet. He wanted me to be a stifled housewife, sitting at home waiting for my husband to return from his business trips, my every step supervised and criticised by my mother-in-law. As the first year of our marriage continued, Parviz began siding with his mother in our disputes and she succeeded in slowly diminishing his feelings towards me. It appeared that I had walked straight from one prison to another.

He once told me in a letter that anything he wrote would be closer to the truth than what I wrote, simply by virtue of him being a man. Questioning the truthfulness of my writing made me doubt our emotional bond. His comments condemned me, suggesting that women cannot be trusted. These views were deeply rooted in his upbringing, of course, but they destabilised our relationship. I wished for the liberal, empathetic man I had first fallen in love with.

Isolation is the perfect word to describe that time of my life. My knowledge of other cultures and languages was non-existent. I had never travelled and my world was that of Iran in the fifties. I was stuck in a city where I knew almost no one, living mostly with a mother-in-law who disapproved of me. Even my own growing body felt alien to me. Yet in that capsule of isolation, I continued writing and nothing mattered more than this. My fingers were always ink stained. Green, usually, because I liked green ink.

When our son was born I started going to Tehran again. At this time my father was usually with his other wife so my mother would help me take care of Kami while I met friends and colleagues. Ironically, for a little while, the family I had tried so hard to escape became my only source of freedom. I had grown up with such pity for my mother, living under my father's dictatorship, and yet by marrying Parviz it appeared I had merely entered another patriarchal set up. And now my mother was the one saving me from being strangled by domesticity. I would always dread going back to Ahvaz and having to put up with the ungraceful comments of my mother-in-law.

Consequently, the trips to Tehran became more frequent and vicious gossip about my behaviour was again reported back to Parviz.

I was writing constantly and felt rewarded by the appreciation of editors and critics, but others were jealous of my free-spirited attitude to life. The middle-class mentality wouldn't accept that a woman could be a wife and mother but also a poet. I had done nothing wrong except pursue my ambitions. I still loved Parviz desperately. I loved how Kami's face lit up at the sight of him, I loved falling into bed with him after Kami had fallen asleep, I loved his smile. I loved sitting with Parviz drinking tea, watching Kami playing in the garden.

But Parviz was becoming increasingly suspicious of me and began to believe what people told him, rather than trust me. We were growing apart.

To stop writing was impossible. To give up writing would be to give up being myself. My poetry was a landslide then, picking up speed, pouring out of my mind and through my pen.

As my writing began to gain recognition, my private life became public property. I was becoming a successful poet, but my marriage was falling apart. Parviz was a traditional man brought up with an unimaginative idea of how a couple should be together. He had known from the start that I was not the same way. At first he must have been attracted to the part of me that wanted to step over boundaries and open locked doors. But perhaps the reality of my rebellion was too much to put up with.

The joy of having built a family life was fading away day by day. I missed the intimate time when the three of us were a team and made day excursions to picnic by the river. Our love was slipping into a void and we became fixated on some ideal version of life that neither of us were able to provide for the other. It was impossible to ask me to stop writing and stay at home, and it seemed impossible to get him to trust me.

I am not trying to make excuses for my own actions or paint myself as an angel. Far from it. As we began to drift apart, I made mistakes and disappointed him. In all my life, there is only one thing I truly regret. It is that I lived up to my husband's fears. I ruined everything, with a joyless affair.

Eventually, I did exactly what Parviz feared I would do.

And then he was right. And then he stopped loving me.

The year of my marriage, 1951, Mohammad Mosaddegh had become prime minister of Iran. He was an advocate of secular democratic government and a keen critic of the Shah. He was an author, a lawyer and an MP who introduced a series of land and tax reforms, but his most audacious reform was the nationalisation of the Iranian oil industry. The largest oil refinery in the world was in Iran and had its own roads, houses, airports and municipal services. Iranian oil had been in the hands of the British since 1913 and British workers did all the skilled jobs with Iranians only hired as labourers. For years before becoming prime minister Mosaddegh had argued that if we took control of our own raw materials we could combat poverty, disease and backwardness among the Iranian people. He had rallied the population, inspiring us to hold onto our cultural identity. I admired him greatly.

In response to the nationalisation of Iranian oil and Mosaddegh becoming prime minister, the British imposed economic sanctions and supported the Anglo-Persian Oil Company's call for a worldwide boycott of Iranian oil. The Americans, who supported the Shah and felt their presence in Iran threatened by Mosaddegh, followed suit and these embargoes sent the Iranian economy into free-fall. The Americans used his links to the Communist Party as an excuse to get rid of him. Three years after he became prime minister, the CIA and MI6 removed Mosaddegh from power and re-installed the monarchy. Mosaddegh was then imprisoned for three years, during which Iranian identity went through a deep crisis.

Two years after the birth of Kami, Parviz and I had reached the end of the line together.

A lonely period of fight and survival lay ahead of me: separation, divorce, a custody battle. My father was ready to help me pay for a lawyer to get custody of Kami but I knew in my heart that Kami would be better off with Parviz and his family, in the environment he'd always known. I loved my son more than anything in the world and for this reason I made the most difficult decision of my life: to allow Parviz custody of him. It was not a lack of love, just self-knowledge. I knew my own faults. I could not provide the stable home that Parviz could.

Having said that, I never for a moment imagined that I was giving up all rights to see my son, or that I would be vilified in his eyes. I couldn't have guessed that Parviz and his family would tell Kami I had abandoned him for poetry and the pursuit of my love life; that I didn't love him. Perhaps Kami was too young to understand exactly what this meant, but he was old enough to be influenced. Everything might have been different if I'd known they would never let me see him. It had not occurred to me that they would be capable of such injustice.

Even if I had fought for him I probably would not have won. The law allows a father to be granted custody of a son from age three and a daughter from age seven, but Parviz and his family argued that I was an incapable mother and went for full custody from the start. Iran's patriarchal, family-oriented society is not kind to divorced women – divorce being considered a great source of shame – let alone to those who are divorcees by the age of nineteen. While a man is granted a divorce just by saying the words 'I want to divorce you' in front of two witnesses, for a woman it is almost impossible to instigate a legal separation. A woman faces complicated bureaucratic hurdles and difficult, often impossible, financial repercussions.

A Muslim *Quadi* (judge) rules over the divorce proceedings and will first try to reconcile the couple before considering granting a divorce. The woman is usually granted *Mehriyeh*, a marriage security fund, which in most cases will not be enough to support her.

Sadly, our divorce became the talk of the town and both our families felt dishonoured by the scandal.

I stayed with my parents in Tehran while the divorce was unfolding but my father's anger stopped me from ever feeling safe, so my mother suggested I live in a little room at the back of the garden, away from the main house. Every time my father saw me he seemed to fly into a rage, and for some reason he seemed to be around more than usual during this period. One evening I happened to walk into their living room when the radio was broadcasting a programme about literature in the background and a distinguished critic compared my work to one of the greatest poets of Persian literature, Mowlana. For a moment in our lamplit room I held the brief hope that my father – a learned, well-read man – might allow himself to be proud of me. Instead he immediately began to scream at my mother, saying it was her fault that I had come to live such a filthy life. My poor mother, who always tried to be kind and understanding, didn't know how to react. She was being condemned for my failures, but not lauded for my successes.

Sometimes I thought that everyone would be happy and relieved if I were to die. I found it difficult to imagine that my existence could bring happiness to anyone.

I played the lottery and hoped that one day I could afford to buy everything for Kami and for myself. I felt powerless. In trying to shake free of convention, I had shaken myself free from all foundations and roots. I was out of control.

During our divorce Kami continued living with Parviz's family and they didn't allow me any visiting rights. I missed my husband and my son. Although Parviz was emotionally brutal, in practical ways he was kind. He did his best to organise for me to have some money in order to survive, and he took care of all Kami's expenses. I still felt a deep love for Parviz and was desperate for his attention as well as the love of our son. I always kept a glimmer of hope in my heart that Parviz would realise how traumatic it was for a mother to be separated from her child and start letting me see him.

Soon after the divorce my first poetry collection was published. At this point I had become a public figure. I was a story; a wild thing growing against the odds between slabs of concrete. A rebel, a divorcee, a poetess.

Prestigious journals were lining up to publish my poems and because I wrote first person accounts of erotic experiences in my poetry, men seemed compelled to slot themselves into the narrative. Sometimes journalists and critics seemed more interested in guessing who the poems were about than in discussing the language or rhythms.

With fame came scrutiny and scandal. Even people I trusted chose to use my fame for their own gain. A prominent poet and literary editor published a story involving a character who has an extra marital affair with a 'song writer'. Everyone assumed the story was about him having an affair with me.

This was an act of absolute treason and deception. I did not have any experience of life. Society, family and friends all watched me closely looking for new opportunities for criticism. My impertinent attitude! Revealing clothes! The kohl on my eyes!

But none of this was important in comparison to being away from my beloved son with no sense of when I might be allowed to see him again. He was my life and all that lived in me. Losing him brought me to the brink of insanity. Being separated from him was like an open wound that tormented me constantly. At night sometimes I held the little red car I'd bought him before I left, but hadn't been allowed to give him. I had wanted him to be left with a good memory of me.

Soon I collapsed under the weight of my strange life. I couldn't face the painful reality any more.

I ended up in the Rezai Psychiatric Clinic in Tehran, suffering from a nervous breakdown. I did not want to exist in my own life any more. I couldn't lift up my head because my neck could not carry the weight of the pain in my mind. I was drained, desperate, faithless. Everyone was ashamed of me, and so my loneliness was engulfing. It had seemed unbearable to continue so the only way to find freedom, was to go to sleep and never wake up.

My room at the clinic was cold and empty. I woke up alone. Who brought me here? My older brother Amir? But where had he gone? Why was nobody saying anything to me? I became impatient and wanted to get out of bed, but then I realised that I was attached to it.

As the weeks went on, I tried to find strength again. I wanted to turn the page and start over. Every day I tried to convince myself that I would be free soon. Sometimes my mother visited, other times my friends. Not Parviz. Not my son. I often dreamed of Kami and woke up aching for his body in my arms.

One day a handsome man appeared in the frame of my hospital doorway. Nader Naderpur was a respected poet with an extraordinary knowledge of foreign literature. When he stood that day in my room, it was like seeing an angel who had come to save me and pluck me from the abyss. He began to pay me regular visits at the hospital, picking up the broken pieces of me that had fallen to the ground and calmly slotting them back together again like a puzzle. He was not oppressive like most men in my life, but instead began to build my confidence. He understood that I needed to be loved, and that love would give me strength to survive. And so he inspired me, and once I was out of hospital we soon became lovers. Over the next year I began to heal and climb out of the void, even while fighting against the people who wanted to knock me back down again.

Although he helped me regain sanity at a difficult time of my life, once I was living normally again our relationship began to peter out. It came to a complete end after a party where Nader accused me of flirting with some of the other guests. He could not bear the fact that other men were interested in me. He was an impulsive person and during this one particular dinner party, he simply stood up and left me then and there. We met only a few times after that.

A different and intriguing world opened up to me when I moved from my parents' to my friend Tousi Hâéri's house. Her ex-husband was one of the most respected literary figures in Iran. We spent hours reading books together. One particularly exciting discovery for me was *The Songs of Bilitis*, a collection of erotic poems written by Pierre Louys and published in Paris in 1894. Louys claimed that the poems were found on the walls of a tomb in Cyprus and had been written by a courtesan named Bilitis who lived at the same time as Sappho in Ancient Greece. Although he pretended to be the translator, he was in fact the author. I found the female perspective on erotic themes, as well as the use of language, reminiscent of some of my own poetry.

I was also taken with the work of Garcia Lorca, the Spanish poet and playwright, who was executed by a right-wing firing squad in 1936 during the Spanish Civil War. Lorca said the only hope for happiness lies in 'living one's instinctual life to the full'. And: 'To burn with desire and to remain silent is the greatest punishment we can inflict on ourselves.'

Although we never performed on stage, a group of us, including Tousi, immersed ourselves in Lorca's 1932 tragedy, *Noces de Sang* (Blood Wedding), about passionate women rebelling against the constraints of society.

I often woke up sweaty and anxious in the night. When I tried to remember my dream it would slip away from me. I would hope to fall asleep again but fail. At this time I was always trying to write articles to earn money, but if I spent too much time on this endeavour I would miss out on writing poems. I wanted to live without depending so heavily on Parviz and my parents for money, but could not find a way of making a living from my poetry.

I missed Parviz and wrote him letters regularly. I had been so protected, but now my life was empty. He had tried so hard to give me what I wanted, but I took it for granted and was now suffering deeply for my betrayal. Parviz always seemed to have such inner stability and control, where I was too emotional. I was the one who did not deserve his love, and now it felt as if I would never be happy again.

I thought of the boiling hot days when we would all go swimming together. I was happy then. I feel lonely, and weighed down by my own stupidity.

Occasionally Kami was allowed to visit my parents, but only without me being there. It was made clear that if we broke this rule then Kami would not be allowed to visit at all. It was important to me that Kami saw my mother because she would tell me how he had grown and how he was developing. He enjoyed being at my parents' house because his cousins would come by frequently and therefore he was never alone like he often was in Ahvaz. He had space to run around my parents' garden.

I felt tired and old and saw myself reaching the end of my life. At age twenty-three, I felt like a sixty-year-old woman. My dream of having a family and simultaneously being a poet had turned out to be a fairy tale. Traditional Iranian families simply cannot accommodate female ambition. From birth, girls are treated as if they were ignorant and incapable while boys are admired simply by virtue of their gender. By turning my back on these expectations, I had shaken off the love of my husband, my father, and quite possibly my son.

Freedom has a high price.

I collected disappointments and wounds.

My father blamed my mother for how I was choosing to live my life. One day when I was visiting them I overheard my father's familiar refrain about how it was her fault I was an idiot who behaved so irresponsibly. He even went as far as to claim that I couldn't possibly be his biological daughter. 'She doesn't even look like me,' he shouted, which was true. He said I was shameful. Outrageous. Impossible.

Usually when my father was like this, she would sit in a corner and cry but this time she answered back in a trembling voice:

'In a country where women are treated as cattle, is it any wonder she rebelled?'

I thought he might hit her. She flinched but he restrained himself with a look of fury in his eyes.

That night, after everyone was asleep, she came to my bed and whispered affectionate and supportive words to me. I listened, keeping quiet while she caressed my hair with fingers hardened by the chores of a housewife.

'You know, sometimes you meet people on your path and you are perfectly aware that your paths are crossing for only a short moment of time,' she said. 'There is no other way to see beyond it. Sometimes encounters have walls around them.'

In 1956 my second collection of poetry was published. But I was like a bird with a broken wing, unable to fly. The clouds would not let me see any more. I was tired and exhausted from trying to be strong in the face of so many calamities. I was constantly holding my breath, swallowing my emotions and bottling up my fears. It felt as if I couldn't release the screams trapped inside me, or say what was in my heart. I was constantly in the public eye, being judged by strangers. There was nobody to protect me or fight my corner. I wanted to feel young and free but instead my entire being was like a scar. And who was there to heal it? The pressure of society was my enemy and it had brought me to the brink of destruction. I couldn't handle life any more. I wanted to live like any other young woman but I wasn't allowed. Strict eyes condemned every step I took.

At this time I had a recurring dream of lying in my childhood bedroom watching scenes from my past play out just beyond the door: the games, recriminations, kisses and false starts that made up the fabric of my life. While watching myself laugh with Parviz in the sitting room or play fight with my brothers in the kitchen, a new door would mysteriously appear in my bedroom where in reality no wall had existed. I would instinctively walk towards it and reach my hand to touch the knob, then turn back to my past one more time to see my books, my siblings, my husband. My warm hand grips the cold metal knob and I open the door. I step forward into a void, leaving everything from my past behind.

It was clear to me that I was going to have another nervous breakdown if I didn't make a dramatic change to my life. I wanted to laugh again. I wanted to fly. I decided to leave Iran.

I believe that meeting Parviz while on my way to get my visa turned out to be a lucky turning point, although it was devastating at the time. Afterwards, his attitude changed.

The morning before I left I did a little last-minute shopping and then headed back to my parents to say goodbye before going to the airport. The last weeks in Tehran had been strange – everyone was kind to me, as if nobody wanted to leave a bad impression on me before my voyage.

I expected to find my parents eating lunch when I got home, but instead I found Kami sitting at the kitchen table with my mother and father. I watched from outside the door for a moment, feeling cold even though it was summer time. My hands were frozen and my eyes were fixed on my beautiful son, who I had not seen in so long. My parents knew I was coming back before going to the airport, so this visit must have been a parting gift from them to me. I caught my mother's eye and offered a small expression of thanks for such a huge act of love. She smiled shyly back at me. I walked over and sat down next to my son. He immediately stared at me and started stroking my face with his little fingers. He did not speak. He looked weak somehow, and too skinny, but he was the sweetest and most loving child on earth. He clearly remembered me. My heart nearly broke. I had been so excited to leave, but now this became a day that was both devastating and elating.

I couldn't eat or drink. After lunch I took him aside and we spread ourselves out on the day bed. He always used to enjoy listening to my stories. Lying there with him resting on my shoulder was an almost unbearable bliss, tinged with terrible sadness. We felt protected by the story in that moment, and I felt protected just by being next to Kami. I had missed him so much. Would he completely forget about me, eventually? How does memory work with children? I caressed his hair and wondered who drew him pictures of elephants, bikes and trains in my absence. Who brushed his hair?

I felt devastated by the idea I was not going to see him for a while. Although I was sad to leave my home, I needed to see light again. I did not leave because I wanted to explore other countries, but to avoid falling deeper into the hole I had been stuck in since the divorce. I needed to find my voice again.

An hour later a friend showed up to drive me to the airport and I tried to restrain my tears. I hoped my mother and father wouldn't get in trouble for allowing me to see Kami. Both my parents had tears in their eyes as I hugged them goodbye. I realised that my father loved me in his way and had brought a great deal of good into my life. I kissed Kami goodbye and gave him the little car I hadn't been able to give him before the divorce.

On that hot July day I cried all the way to the airport as my home city sped by outside the window. I was leaving everything I knew and loved. A sense of the unknown overwhelmed and excited me.

The friend who had accompanied me to the airport was surprised I was boarding a cargo plane, but I wasn't ashamed. For someone who was brought up sleeping with blankets meant for soldiers, and being dragged outside to exercise first thing every morning regardless of heat or snow, a cargo plane was the natural choice.

There were five passenger seats on the plane, two doubles and one single. I was sat next to an English-speaking man who spoke angry foreign words that I guessed were admonishing staff for the plane's delay. I was pleased he didn't speak Farsi so we wouldn't need to communicate. Once on the plane I felt almost paralysed, hermetically sealed. I wanted to close my eyes and ears and not engage with anyone.

As soon as the plane started to roll, so again did the tears down my cheeks. It was real; I was leaving. I tried to cry silently, wiping my face with my hands, but my travel companion couldn't help but notice. Although he motioned to the *Manual of English Language* peeking out of my bag, suggesting we might use it to communicate, once the engine had started the loud noise made it impossible to talk or hear each other anyway, even if we had spoken the same language.

From the window, Tehran was getting smaller and smaller, then it vanished from my view.

Part Two

I open the window to inhale the scent of the sea. Salt air and pine trees flood my little Beirut hotel room as I sit and write. This window fills my room with light as the horizon flickers in the distance. I love windows – from the safety of a secure space, they offer a glimpse into another landscape and another life. A window can spark the imagination.

While the Mediterranean Sea glitters in the distance, inside my hotel room it is cramped and crowded with too much furniture for the small space. There's a chaise longue, a bed, a small desk and to the right of the desk, my image is reflected in a wall mirror. I look pale and dirty and tired; I must have a bath before going down to dinner but do not want to stop writing. I feel liberated, as if all my worries and problems have floated towards the horizon. I find the continuous movement of the waves soothing.

I have been writing another long letter to Parviz, who for the last months has been writing me back and even sending drawings from Kami. It occurred to me that perhaps he had actually allowed Kami to see me on my last day in Tehran, that it had been a gift. These letters and pictures made me both melancholy and joyful at the same time. I needed them, but on the other hand they reminded me of all my mistakes. My life is intertwined with Parviz and in a way our bond only gets stronger with time. Being far away and detached gave me strength. I found refuge in my own thoughts and enjoyed writing letters home. I had always loved writing to Parviz – even when we were married I would write him letters. But now, when we are so far from each other, I desperately want him to know how much I cherished the life we'd had together.

When I first left Tehran I'd stayed in Munich with my eldest brother Amir, who had moved before the *coup d'etat* in 1953 to complete his medical studies. Amir lived in a tiny apartment and was already integrated into the literary and political scenes. We shared our passion for literature and I was looking forward to learning German in order to read German poetry. I plunged immediately into the city's intellectual life, visiting museums and galleries and libraries. Amir and I decided to translate our favourite poems from a recently published anthology selected by London-based exile Eric Singer. They were mostly written by poets who were exiled or escaped from Nazi Germany.

After a few months in Munich, I travelled to Rome. At first I didn't love the city. In some ways Rome reminded me of Tehran, although the people seemed much less friendly. Walking around the street after 7 pm was not recommended for women alone – Italian men would stop their cars and make comments or whistle when they saw you. I studied Italian and worked on a translation of two poetry books from Italian into Farsi. I spent most of my time thinking about poetry and if a day went by that I didn't dedicate to language then I considered that a lost day.

Living in Rome awoke in me a deep respect for the past and its preservation. One day I found myself in the square next to the train station staring at an old stone wall that had remained intact whilst glass and metal surfaces grew around it. It surely would have been easier to knock down this wall to make space for sleek and modern infrastructure, but the wall endured. As people rushed and jostled around me in the busy square outside the station, it was clear that the old and the new became only more beautiful when balanced against each other. Ancient walls such as this one are bridges to the future. In Rome I began to recognise the importance of being attached to the past, while still looking forward.

One strange night, after hearing guttural noises in the hotel room next door to mine, I lay in bed for a moment wondering what the source could be. It sounded almost animal, like a creature's dying howl. When I stepped out of my room to see if I could help, half of the hotel guests from the fourth floor were congregating in the hallway. Eventually they broke into the room next to mine and found a small woman lying on the floor next to an open suitcase full of underwear, torn socks, coloured paper and children's books. There was also a picture of Jesus, an artificial eye and several empty packets of pills. She had taken an overdose and was dying on the carpet, slipping in and out of consciousness. I stood there frozen. Had she travelled from another city or country specifically to check into a hotel room and die alone? What brought her to this point of no return? Who had been cruel to her? In what way had she suffered?

I will never have the answer. I tried to help but others were stronger and they brought her downstairs. It seemed to me that her body was not treated with the respect a human being deserves, but I was shooed away from the scene. All I know is that she didn't survive and died that night. I wonder what happened to her books, her clothes, her scraps of coloured paper.

I had reached the end of a chapter and was beginning another life now, which felt full of hope. However, like an old wall balancing the new, I realised that I could not fight or ignore the sorrow that was my past. It was part of me. It could not be knocked down, or run from.

In my bag, I carried all kinds of memories from school and pieces of paper that friends had written or scribbled for me. There was a sadness that I encountered everywhere I went, but that sadness was in me and reflected my own perception.

During this trip to Europe I realised how different it would have been if I'd been born in a free society where respect for women is normal. If I'd started my career in a society where men and women were all treated like human beings and judged on their minds and character rather than their gender. I had never felt so calm and free as I did in those nine months. I was finally getting some distance from the suffocating world I grew up in. I was opening my arms to new energy and hope.

Part Three

The small balcony door is left half open as if someone had just escaped through it. I am lying in my bed looking out of the window at the old fig tree. Above it, dawn is once again creeping across the sky. Different species of birds converse, sharing the secrets they have witnessed during the night. The dawn begins to fade into light.

It is hot and I am half covered with a *shamad*, a thin cotton cloth used in the summer. The leaves outside my window are not still. A quiet breeze caresses them like fingers through my thick hair. Am I asleep or awake? I can hear the arrival of the morning with all the sounds of birds and nature coming from different sides of my garden. I open my eyes.

The month of August is known to be the hottest month of the year in Tehran, day and night. My house is in the northern part of the capital where it is cooler due to the numerous small rivers and green spaces. The city has spread out since my childhood and some residential areas are located right at the foot of the chain of Mount Alborz.

I close my eyes again but sleep has left my house. Instead I turn and grab my cigarettes from a pile of books by my bed, and light one with a match. At age twenty-five, I have reached an important place amongst the Iranian literati. The themes I write about make the male-dominated world of poetry uncomfortable, but I don't pay attention to their criticism. I have found my own language and style. My last collection of poetry was even mentioned in Russia recently, in a lecture about world literature. I write poems to survive. My everyday life is the core of my poems. I live my poems and my poems live my life.

I look at my hands now, and they are still smoking while I lie in bed. I am slowly reaching quarter of a pack of cigarettes before waking up properly. I get carried away by my own thoughts and lose the notion of time easily.

It is bright now in my room and I need to get up. I still feel yesterday's night of bliss and caresses on the sheets that surround me. I can still smell his breath and his skin. His entire being stays with me long after he has left our embrace. I keep reviving those hours and calling them back to my mind.

I stir, and consider getting out of bed. Today I will have Darjeeling tea leaves from Mongolia mixed with pink and orange rose petals. Each morning my choice of tea informs my day. If I ever miss this sacred routine, I lack energy the rest of the day.

Sometimes, I get bored with my own thoughts. I need to urgently wipe them out of my mind. The heavenly voices of the opera *Fidelio* play as I get dressed for work. It is soothing like a medicine and transports me to another era.

In a couple of hours I will see the man I love again.

When I returned from Europe a year ago, I immediately started searching for work and was able to find a position writing regularly for a free-thinking literary magazine called *Ferdowsi*. It didn't pay well but I enjoyed writing articles about my trip to Europe, and my childhood, and poetry. The editor of the magazine tried to seduce me but I had returned home to Tehran with clarity and purpose. All I cared about was poetry and my son now. Parviz allowed me to see Kami occasionally, which was wonderful.

Some mutual friends kindly put me forward to interview for a secretarial position at a film and photography studio run by a successful film director, photographer and short story writer. Ebrahim had gained fame with his first feature film about the *coup d'etat* that toppled Mossaddegh in 1953. Ebrahim was known for being a leader in his community of artists, as well as a colossal intellect and a member of the communist party, Tudeh.

The Tudeh party was the pulse of the political resistance to the authoritative regime at the time. The British Ambassador called it the only coherent political force in the country – it appealed to a broad group and managed to have eight candidates elected in the Majlis parliament in 1944. The group had played an important role in supporting the Mossaddegh's campaign to nationalise the Anglo-Persian Oil Company and had organised a series of strikes which had resulted in two hundred of its members being arrested. Once Reza Shah was forced into exile in South Africa, however, many of these prisoners were released and the movement started to flourish.

For the interview I wore my favourite black skirt with a slim-cut jumper. The skirt was the perfect length, just above the knee, and had a small cut at the back. The jumper had a flattering yet demure neck line. I covered this with a light coat I'd bought in Italy, although to my irritation I couldn't find exactly the right shoes. I wanted to look elegantly casual so the heels couldn't be too high, but flat shoes would look ugly.

I chain smoked cigarettes on the pavement outside the studio, tottering in uncomfortable borrowed shoes, before entering the building. My palms were sweaty and my skirt felt too tight as I was led through the corridors. It was early in the morning so the building was still, with camera equipment and photographic negatives abandoned on desks ready to be picked up again soon.

When I was ushered into the boss's office he looked up from a notepad on his desk and motioned for me to sit down. He was an attractive man with a mane of dark hair and a high forehead. His face was expressive and his eyes shone in the early morning light that streamed through his office window. I'd done some research into him before the interview so knew he was born in Shiraz in 1922 where his father owned the local newspaper, and that from an early age he had been exposed to an artistic community. He was married to his cousin, with whom he had a daughter and a son.

'This job is mostly concentrated on filing and answering phone calls for the office,' he said calmly. 'We have many photographers and film makers working in the studio and your work will be to assist everyone with logistics.' He stared at me and I nodded. 'Just to be clear from the beginning,' he said, 'this job has nothing to do with writing poetry.'

Strangely enough, I liked this confrontational moment and didn't feel bothered at all. The way he spoke was totally disarming. I answered quickly:

'I am ready to start anytime,' I said.

This was my first encounter with the man who would change my life.

In the months after this brief, pragmatic conversation, I became increasingly inspired by his intelligence, creativity and generosity of spirit. He was an openminded intellectual, at ease in different cultures and languages, so working at his side was a powerful education. Just by watching him and his colleagues I began to gain an understanding of photographic composition and visual storytelling. It was a privilege to learn from Ebrahim and his colleagues and with their help the boundaries of my job slowly changed from basic administrative tasks into researching new projects and helping with production.

In my spare time I stayed at the office and learned the basics of film editing. The work was so fascinating that I didn't even realise how many hours a day I was at the office. We became close. He listened to my opinions, and we argued about art and philosophy.

Although integrating into the studio team was difficult at first, I soon became part of their creative and technical work. Parallel to that, I decided to take some extra courses on film directing in the evenings. My first big project was working on both the filming and editing of a short documentary about a fire that lasted for two months in the oilfields of Khuzestan Province. We treated it as a duel between man and nature.

We were commissioned by a Canadian company. At the time, there were a large number of foreign engineers who had moved to Abadan and Ahvaz to be involved in the oil refinery industry. A whole new infrastructure was built to maximise the production and many British engineers occupied important managerial positions. The studio earned most of its income by making documentaries for foreign companies, which allowed us to create niche artistic films.

The team at our studio was made up of a mixed pot of people from diverse professional backgrounds; there was a film director recently freed from prison as well as directors who had studied and developed their careers in foreign countries. We also had poets, translators and photographers, so the studio was fertile ground for new ideas and artistic expression. The success of Ebrahim's company was due to his creative mind as well as his leadership as an entrepreneur and businessman.

I continued publishing poems. Ebrahim was an infinite source of inspiration. He gave me the confidence to write without inhibitions, to submerge myself in photography, and to start working on documentaries the company had been commissioned to make. My creativity was blooming on all fronts.

I couldn't help falling in love with him. It was unstoppable, magnetic. He accepted me and loved me with all the scars on my body and soul.

The man I loved was happily married and lived a normal family life with his two children. He was able to separate the two lives, and two loves. I lived my life independently and tried to accept our love where it surfaced. I was amazed that he managed to compartmentalise when these two parts of his life were so burningly close. Ebrahim had bought me a house just ten minutes' drive from his own. His family house had a traditional wall surrounding the property with a rivulet, called a 'joob', running along one side. From far away you could see a cedar of Lebanon tree and Persian ironwoods reaching towards the sky above that wall.

My house was also in the Darrus Area. The front garden had a pathway through it scented with flowers on every side. At the end of the path was a small 1930s modernist house, not at all like the traditional houses where I was brought up. On the ground floor was a living room and two large bay windows opening on to a veranda with steps leading down to a back garden with a fig tree in it. Upstairs there were two bedrooms, one with a small balcony. It was the most beautiful little house I could possibly imagine. There were windows everywhere, even on the staircase, and the house filled with light each morning.

Part Four

A few weeks ago Ebrahim insisted I attend a party at his house. A couple of times a year, a grand gathering of Iran's literati takes place there and everyone hopes for an invitation. I was invited, of course, but obviously felt uncomfortable with the idea of being a guest in the home of my lover's wife. It seemed impossible that I would stay calm and detached in such a scenario, and anyway my presence would cause unnecessary discomfort for her. I was acutely aware that while fighting for my place as an independent woman I was depriving another of her marital stability. It was a knot that could not be unravelled. Ebrahim's solution was simply to live the life he needs to live and hope that his family will come to accept me, but I feel constantly guilty for our love.

I was sitting at home on my bed reading an article that had just appeared about my poetry, when I heard the doorbell. I wondered if it was a guest for Ebrahim's party arriving at my house by mistake. I usually held informal gatherings on Friday nights, where friends and colleagues could come and go as they pleased throughout the evening. I liked to invite people from different backgrounds and professions to inject energy into the evenings. There was always food and drink on offer, often out in the garden when the weather was fine. Everyone was encouraged to discuss controversial issues and challenge each other intellectually. Often the evenings would end with a poetry reading, a guest playing the Tar, and sometimes I would compose a poem especially for the occasion.

I assumed everyone would know there was no gathering tonight, since most people would be going to Ebrahim's house. I got off the bed and went to the intercom.

'It's me,' said a voice I recognised as belonging to Rahman, the studio's driver. I walked barefoot through the garden, inhaling the scent of my full bloom Roses of Isfahan, and Rahman stood hesitantly in the doorway.

'Ebrahim Agha insists that you join the party tonight,' he smiled. 'The guests are beginning to arrive and he sent me to drive you.'

Rahman was such a kind man. He had a protective energy and I felt swayed by the idea of Ebrahim wanting me by his side. Standing there amongst the smell of roses and evening air I suddenly felt tempted and my resolve crumbled away. Ebrahim wanted me there with him, and the desire to make him happy became stronger than my will.

'Give me fifteen minutes to get ready,' I said to Rahman.

I went upstairs to my room and took a black dress out of my wardrobe, pulling it over my head and then brushing my hair. I put on lipstick and was ready.

When we arrived at the party Ebrahim's wife was at the entrance so we had to greet each other politely. I sensed the icy gaze of other guests fall on me. I felt like a dangerous animal who had just been released into an arena, with all eyes upon me. It was frightening and a chill went down my spine. I had an intuition this was going to be a critical moment in my life. I picked up a strong drink while scanning the room for Ebrahim. I hadn't had much to eat that day so this first drink gave me some confidence but also made me a bit tipsy.

At the sight of Ebrahim across the room an immediate happiness invaded my entire body. My face lit with joy and I could have screamed his name out loud. He approached me and smiled.

He took me around the party and introduced me to a few writers. We stood with different groups of friends for a while, drinking and laughing but often glancing over at each other. My group's conversation turned to definitions of the bourgeois, and began to get quite heated. I argued that possessions do not necessarily make one bourgeois: if you own a Rolls Royce you are not necessarily materialistic or conventional. To be bourgeois was a state of mind.

This group of men vehemently disagreed with my view, saying that exterior signs of wealth such as clothing and cars are not befitting of someone who calls themselves an intellectual. This was a thinly veiled attack on my poetry and relationship.

I was a little drunk and may have suggested that one of the participants in this debate had a bourgeois state of mind even if he didn't have the corresponding middle-class lifestyle. He disagreed:

'How can you stand here with the rank of half-hostess, in this big garden in front of this fancy house, and call us bourgeois?' he said.

I felt a dagger in my heart but tried to remain calm, sipping my drink. I was speechless and didn't know how to defend myself. I was in pain and looked around for Ebrahim, but he had moved to the other side of the room. I was alone and felt crushed by the weight of the moment. It was hard to keep my composure and hide all my anger and frustration. Injustice and discrimination enrage me. My greatest wish is that Iranian women will one day be free from the men who adore only themselves, and rule without justice.

Then another man, a family friend of Ebrahim's, reached over and took my raincoat out of my hands. He tore off the label from the neck.

'Here you are, Madame,' he said. 'I have removed the bourgeois label from your coat.'

He was trying to be funny but only showed himself to be vulgar and belligerent. I laughed as if I were unconcerned by his actions, but in truth I was angry. The men were showing their jealousy in a disgraceful manner. Their game of mockery revealed their limitations. Their attacks condemned my relationship with Ebrahim. The men were frustrated that a woman could become a famous poet when poetry had always been considered male territory. How dare she?

I don't know why I didn't leave the party earlier. I tried to calm myself with more drinks, which didn't do me any favours. I couldn't think straight. I got trapped and carried on drinking, hanging on at the party for no reason that could make me happy. Maybe, I wanted to feel Ebrahim's presence. I can't recall in what sort of a state I left the party but I remember being one of the last guests to leave. I was driven back home by Rahman.

The day afterwards I looked in the mirror and cried. Who is the woman in that mirror? I admit to myself – I have made many mistakes. But who can say that he or she has done everything right for their entire life? I dare to face my mistakes, although it is a painful act.

I was so dependent on him. I lived in a house that I couldn't afford myself. Being a woman poet in the fifties and sixties in Iran was far from a lucrative metier. I had to finance my own print runs, as other poets did. No one could afford to live on their talent in creative writing. Furthermore, the salary I received from the Golestan studios wasn't enough for me to afford to live in a nice house in the residential part of northern Tehran. Before I met Ebrahim I had lived in a small apartment and still depended on the money I received sometimes from my ex-husband. Total financial independence was a dream I wasn't close to reaching.

Part Five

Part Five

I keep staring at the white ceiling above my bed. It is quite unusual for Ebrahim and I to remain apart for more than twenty-four hours but this week we both had a tremendous work load. When Ebrahim approached me at the office yesterday, I intuitively knew that he would say we couldn't meet that night. It hit me hard. A cold sweat surfaced on my skin. Later, when we were working with colleagues, I moved my lips towards him and whispered in his ear:

'All is emptiness without you.'

I am tortured by how nothing can possibly stay the same and relationships change due to events, circumstances, mistakes, misunderstandings or a lack of attention. I don't know where I stand with Ebrahim today.

Between happiness, passion and bliss, we have blazing arguments emanating from my frustration and desperation. I need to be held in his arms until dawn and the impossibility of our closeness builds up immense inner tension in me. That is why any small issue ends up in shouts and screams.

We have to put up with condemnation from our circle of acquaintances. I am portrayed as the immoral woman who entered Ebrahim's life and engaged in a relationship with a married man against all rules and tradition. It is almost impossible to survive as a divorced woman in this judgemental society and every day I feel a bit more powerless. The only way to save myself is to find refuge in poetry.

I miss Kami badly, but since Ebrahim and I have been together Parviz has cooled towards me again. He no longer writes me letters as he did when I was travelling in Europe, and he does not let me see Kami. The urge to be near my son is a visceral energy though, pulling me into dangerous territory. What would happen if I appeared at his school gates one day? Would he run into my arms? Or was he angry? Would he ignore me? I found it difficult to imagine what my son's spontaneous reaction would be and one time I impulsively travelled to Ahvaz to meet him coming out of school. I knew it was a bad idea but I needed to see what would happen. I'd been dreaming of Kami for so long. I wanted to tell him that I wasn't an evil mother who abandoned her son for the sake of poetry, but an unfulfilled mother who couldn't fight the will of his father's family. I wanted to tell him that I loved him more and more each day, even though I didn't see him; that he was part of my day-to-day life even if I wasn't part of his.

That day though, Parviz was at the entrance to the school and he refused to let me see Kami. I fainted on the pavement.

Perhaps it was selfish of me. My son had a routine. He had people to care for him and love him. He didn't need me. Later, I wrote a poem for him describing my wish to one day hold him in my arms again.

Tonight is another lonely night, lying in a cold bed. The traces of our passion are washed away. I recall your eyes while you spoke about our love and yet I don't believe it is real because I can't touch 'love' with my lips and fingers. My life is split in two. The joyous days and nights when we are together and embrace for hours. Then the others, when we are not together but far from each other like different planets hovering somewhere in the vast universe. The sun arrives with you and the night falls without you. You are the orientation of my life, my calendar. My centre of creativity is nurtured by your gaze.

The world outside my head seems full of noise and joy and yet my life feels empty. I ask myself whether it is worth going on? One day I find myself high with happiness and the next day I plunge underneath the surface of the earth. It is uncontrollable. The emotions take over and rise up in their unpredictable pattern. Reason loses its fight. I am in an isolated place where I have to fight to be able to love and be loved. I am desperate and weak, with no intention of pursuing happiness. A few weeks ago, I swallowed a whole container of sleeping pills as a solution to my pains, but after spending time in the Alborz hospital, I knew I had to fight to stay alive because I did not want to give up the people I love.

My complaint is rooted in the discrimination between men and women.

My wish is that my work brings freedom to Iranian women and allows them to share the same rights as men.

My question is: 'Will Iranian men who grew up in a patriarchal system, ever stop being so selfish and self-indulgent?'

I hear the postman arriving. I am excited to see who has written to me. My mother, my sister, my brother, my son? The letter is from my younger brother Ferydoun who lives in Germany and has made a career for himself as a singer and song writer. He has sent me some of his recent poems. He is very talented and I wish he would translate my poems into German.

I start to read his letter. There is an undercurrent of nostalgia about Tehran running through his lines. I have to keep warning him of the dangerous pseudo-intellectual climate here. He is better off staying in Germany and continuing to build his career. At least he is in a place where people are not so narrow-minded and judgemental. I have earned so little compared to the press exposure I've had.

Ferydoun and I have always been quite open towards each other. He was never shy of showing me how sensitive he was. I vividly remember when he glued his tearful eyes on our father, the moment my father announced his departure from the family. It was a painful experience for both of us and we expressed it in totally opposite ways, although we were both devastated. Ferydoun had to show his emotions and couldn't stop his tears. For an Iranian boy, this revealed a true sign of weakness. But years later, when Ferydoun felt secure in his work and career, he acknowledged that real emotions were the source of creativity for writing poems. His homosexuality was always going to get in the way of his success in a traditional society like Iran. He was different and therefore the best place for him was not in a country that condemns anyone not perceived as 'normal'. No escape for Ferydoun, nor for me.

Part Six

I am sitting in the shadow of a willow tree in the Bababaghi Hospice, a leper colony outside Tabriz. Children are playing all sorts of different outdoor games in the sunshine and I am watching them. During this twelve-day visit, I have learned new definitions for common words. Beauty and ugliness are not opposites. Neither are joy and pain. In beauty there is ugliness and in ugliness, beauty. They can't exist without each other. There are over four hundred people living in this leper colony, cut off from mainstream society even though a cure for leprosy had now been discovered.

A few months ago Ebrahim and I met with a man from the Society for Aid to Lepers. His message was: the government and its medical system have failed to address the problem of the leper community and this social neglect needs to be stopped. His idea was to make a film to break down the audience's fear about leprosy and awaken the government's sense of responsibility. It was a cry for help.

He described how leprosy is often called a 'living death' and those affected have traditionally lived isolated lives in poverty. For hundreds of years, lepers have had to live with fear and rejection. Continuous research since the 1870s has led to the first anti-leprosy drug being discovered in the 1930s, yet the stigma attached to the disease remains. They are seen as unclean, almost inhuman, despite the fact that there is now a cure for the disease. The Bababaghi was the first leprosarium in Iran. In the last decades of the Qajar period, Bababaghi was used as hunting grounds for the crown prince of Tabriz. In 1933, five hectares of this land was allocated to become a leper colony under the direction of the public health administration. In the beginning people from a nearby village supported the colony with donations but slowly this support faded and the people were left totally segregated from the rest of the province.

Now four hundred Lepers live as outcasts there. As the man spoke about these people I immediately felt connected to them and knew that if this project was handled with understanding and courage, it could mark a breakthrough for an abandoned and forgotten community. For me it was clear from the beginning that this film would be a metaphor for the society we live in. I believed the message could work to illuminate questions about what is perceived as 'normal' and 'beautiful' in Iran. Ebrahim asked if I would lead this project, and I jumped at the chance.

My passion was so strong that I ignored the fact that leprosy could be contagious. This was to be my first opportunity to work as a director and I was going to give my whole heart to it.

I gathered a team of four, all of whom were willing to take on this challenge. Ninety-five per cent of people are believed to have immunity to leprosy pathogens, and leprosy is not an incurable disease any more, but there was still a risk. Leprosy is spread through the cough or nasal fluid of an infected person, and can incubate for between five and twenty years before becoming symptomatic.

On a misty morning we took the train towards Northern Iran. The journey was long but very beautiful. The scenery in Azerbeidjan was a feast for the eyes with its seventeen rivers and two lakes. There is also a small chain of mountains in the north of Tabriz, including the majestic Ag Dag. In those rich volcanic soils, medicinal herbs and tulips are planted.

My aspiration was for the film to work on numerous levels. Although it would be about the leper colony of Bababaghi, the film would also explore the fact that great trouble and suffering is caused when we reject certain parts of ourselves and bury our unwelcome feelings, rather than facing up to our problems and searching for a solution. The story of a community being rejected due to a lack of access to proper medical help would draw wider attention to how societies are willing to condemn anything that is different to themselves, rather than to confront their fears of the other. Our aim was to change the negative and 'unclean' image attached to leprosy and allow our audience to see the sufferers as human beings just like them.

My worry was that the community would not react well to an outsider penetrating their world and putting it on film. I knew that the first step would be to take still images so they could slowly get accustomed to us and our cameras. We would have to prove ourselves to be friends, eager to understand rather than to judge them, and hopefully they would see that we could offer them a way to share something of themselves with the outside world. Perhaps they would not want to share themselves, but that was a question I would only be able to answer when we arrived. I could only hope that they would open up to me.

Upon arrival at the train station, a little van from Bababaghi colony was waiting to drive us to the location. As the gates opened and our van drove through into the grounds, my heart was beating so loud that I thought everyone would hear its rhythm. I wasn't afraid but knew that a great challenge was waiting for me. I was twenty-seven and this was my first chance to direct a film.

We were given a few rooms in the hospice, in the part dedicated to visitors. Some European health workers apparently spent time there, but we didn't meet any during our visit. After we unpacked we were invited to the main building, which was the centre of the community and housed prayer rooms, a kitchen, a sitting room, medical facilities and the main offices. It had large corridors and high ceilings because it used to be a royal hunting lodge. That first afternoon we walked around and tried not to stare at any of the lepers we encountered. They all looked at us intently though. We didn't carry our cameras because we wanted to engage with the people directly. We wanted to create an atmosphere of trust and cooperation where no one would feel threatened or looked down upon.

I had prepared many plans on how we would begin, but after walking around that first afternoon I revised them all. Instead of sticking to any sort of script, we would dedicate our time to meeting and engaging with these people, and see where this led us. I was inspired by French New Wave cinema, which is all about radical experimentation with editing and expressing social upheaval in a documentary style. I decided our aim would be to create an atmosphere of trust and cooperation, while using portable equipment to be flexible about how we told the story.

In the morning, there was eerie quiet. Only the birds were singing. This silence was powerful, and it was how I wanted to begin the film.

At first I made still portraits, focussing intently on individual people. I hoped to use these shots in the film, in a fragmented way. It didn't take long before they allowed me to film intimate scenes of their everyday life: a woman washing a baby, a young girl holding a doll and being pushed in a wheelbarrow, adults playing board games with stones or applying mascara.

Because of Kami, I was very focused on the children's behaviour and life in the colony. How different were these children to Kami? Kids in Bababaghi were like kids anywhere – they played with whatever they could find whether it was a stick, a crutch, a car or a ball. They liked wearing hats, perhaps to give them a sense of identity as well as protection. They kick a ball up in the air with their feet, trying to stop it from touching the floor – the same game played by children all over the world.

Our film crew had to commit to intense inner work in order to understand the true essence of the infected patients. We needed to quickly move beyond aesthetics and any small gesture of disgust or fear from our crew would have been a disaster. Day after day, due to the gradual closeness we developed with the people, new possibilities appeared. It was difficult to plan ahead so we had to be spontaneous. I worked intuitively, judging each moment and each scene as it appeared around me. The biggest decision came at an early stage when I decided to let the camera sail through the community and pick up details without imposing a story. Two crucial focal points of the film would be in negotiating the distance between the film and the audience, and the audience and the community.

I plan that in the background there will be different voices: one reading the old testament, one reading the Koran, one saying some facts, and me reading some poems. These voices will accompany the visual images and reveal things that cannot be directly said.

The first voice will appear while the screen is still black. 'There is no shortness of ugliness in the world,' the voice will say. 'If man closed his eyes to it, there would be even more. But man is a problem solver. On this screen will appear an image of ugliness ... a vision of pain no caring human being should ignore. To wipe out this ugliness and to relieve the victims ... is the motive of this film and the hope of its makers.'

This darkness will set the mood of isolation, before the viewer is plunged through the closed door into the life beyond. This is a film about people living far from us, disconnected from society and out of reach from most people's understanding. Blackness will be a leitmotiv that threads and echoes between different scenes. These voids will be moments of imposed contemplation, before the audience is allowed access to something new.

There is an expression in Farsi that says, 'Beyond black there is no colour.'

I have in mind that the first scene will be an image I took of a girl looking intently at herself in the mirror. Her direct gaze shows a fearlessness, and a desire to face life directly. She does not flinch or falter. A man keeps singing at random intervals in the background without being seen on camera, which adds a further haunting quality to the moment. She is all of us; we are all the same. We all cry, laugh, sleep, blush. That is what I want to capture in this documentary.

Another of my most memorable scenes is a woman combing another woman's hair while preparing for a wedding. The important details in life are the same for them and us. It is heart wrenching to witness how much beauty exists in each of these people, all while they are classified as ugly and cast out from the wider world. The divisions that we impose on humanity are subjective and unfair. We are all humans with feelings, dreams and aspirations. We need to look beyond our differences and learn to be thoughtful and humble.

Despite being confined by their geography, poverty and health, the members of this community were more open-minded than I expected.

We were excited to be invited to a wedding. It could have been a wedding celebration in any village in the province: the sound of drums and laughter, men playing guitars and flutes while a woman sung and danced and another carried a tray full of food on her head.

The joy of the event spoke through the music. They played a flute made of bamboo, a drum made of fish skin, and long necked string instruments called *tars*. I focused on one of the young women dancing with a scarf in each hand, turning them around and around. Although we were filming in black and white, the scene was so full of energy that you could almost see the colours of the food and the clothes.

There was such a vast love for life on display. They had been rejected by wider society and despite this rejection they maintained their belief and hope. They had no fear of being judged because they had already been judged and condemned. They could be purely themselves.

When two hands appeared and took the bride's veil aside her face appeared beneath with painted rosy cheeks, covered with jewellery. The groom put his arms around her and turned his face towards the guests. I was honoured to be able to share this profound moment with them. There was such poetry in their movements and expressions. I felt included in their joy and began dancing with them.

I film silence. Hands move some stones in an unidentified game and my voice breaks the quiet: 'Remember that my life is wind?' I say. 'And you have condemned me to idleness.'

A blind man trails his finger along the side of a building to orientate himself.

The sun shines. Children look out of windows, and men smoke on the patio.

A nurse pushes a patient down a long corridor to the infirmary and the camera focusses on particular parts of the human body: eyes, mouths, fingers, toes. The viewer feels the pain of these patients, even though they do not scream.

The distribution of medicine is a ceremonial act. One by one their names are read out and they proceed calmly to the front to be handed their medicine.

A leader reads from the Koran. People pray together, yet each person is speaking intimately to God almighty.

A man whistles outside the main building, and slowly the crowd walks towards him carrying trays and bowls. They sit on the floor to eat their rice with a spoon.

A camera films from inside a window, looking out. There is an alley with trees on both sides and a person is slowly approaching, using crutches. Although it is a long way to walk, he does not falter. He is handicapped but this will not stop him from living, playing, and feeling alive.

Yesterday morning I filmed at a school in central Bababaghi. I was nervous about how the children would react when a stranger showed up in their classroom so I made sure to be early in order to get a sense of the space and set up our cameras.

The children varied in age between six and fifteen years old and I explained to them what my film was about, telling them that they were free to be part of it or leave if they found the idea disturbing. They all chose to be a part of the project and as their lessons commenced some glanced nervously at the camera and others ignored it altogether. I had been so worried about intimidating them, but they did not seem remotely self-conscious in front of the camera. They were spontaneous and attentive with dreamy eyes. Their expressions of avid concentration were beautiful to film. I knew that these children would convince any viewer of how much was shared by those inside and outside the colony. Some children read their lessons in a clumsy way; others answered their teacher's questions with confidence. Light flowed in to the classroom. There was constant background noise as the children hummed, sang or snapped their fingers.

On our final day of filming we were in the classroom again. The teacher came up with questions for pupils to answer:

'Why do we have to care for our mothers and fathers?' asked the teacher, pointing at a student.

'I don't know, I don't have parents,' the student answered.

'Name a few things that are ugly,' the teacher said.

'Hands, feet, head,' a student responded.

'Name a few beautiful things,' the teacher said.

Some students looked at each other. One kept moving and laughing nervously. Another looked like he was concentrating on the question but didn't speak. Finally one boy, who was around eight years old, put his hand up and said:

'Moon, sun, flower, games.'

Some students started to laugh but the one who had spoken smiled serenely, knowing that he had expressed the truth. I was speechless and just repeated his poetic words to myself silently while staring at the boy. The same beautiful things existed for him as for everyone else.

These four words changed both our lives. I felt not only affection, but awe.

At that precious and unforgettable moment, I had to stop and bring the camera down in order to ask what the boy's name was, but he didn't reply.

Instead he smiled shyly, as if perhaps he had forgotten his name. There was an instant feeling of affection between us. I knew straightaway that I would try to adopt him and take him back to Tehran with me, not out of a feeling of charity but because of an immediate and strong human connection. He brought the stars and moon, the beauty of the universe and made it accessible to everyone. It felt as if he could be my son, Kami, yet he was so different from Kami. He was the sun and moon and flowers and games. His name was Hossein.

Hossein Mansouri's parents accepted my offer and I adopted him. The film finished with a black door appearing on-screen, drawing to a close our brief view of the Bababaghi community, but for me the story continued because Hossein was now part of my life.

Part Seven

On the train back to Tehran, it was cold and we were all huddled in one compartment. We had given the last of our money to the community and so took the train without a spare coin in our pockets. It was getting dark and we couldn't see the beautiful landscape out of the window. Hossein's warm presence and inquisitive eyes made me feel snug despite the freezing air. I'm not sure he really understood the adventure he was embarking on, or that he was leaving the only community he'd ever known.

I embraced my little boy for a long time. He was my new son, one that I could love and cherish every day. He knew nothing beyond the leper colony and I did my best to make him feel safe as we left it behind. Of course I wondered if I was doing the right thing, separating a child from his parents. I knew first-hand how hard it is to be separated from your child. Yet by taking him away I would be able to give him everything he needed: healthcare, education, clothes, toys and books.

I had fallen in love with his expressive eyes. When he said those four words in the classroom, he'd touched my heart.

I would dedicate myself to the role of mother, one that I desperately wanted to experience. I would love him unconditionally, and protect him forever.

As soon as I got to Tehran, I decided to write daily letters to Hossein's father. I promised to keep him aware of his son's life and development.

Getting used to our new life together was challenging for both of us. I was not used to having someone around who sees me all the time, while I was writing or being emotional or talking to myself. He witnessed all the ups and downs of my life. He was extremely sensitive and often looked worried for me, or as if he wanted to protect me. Sometimes I would take him to my parents' house and sometimes I would keep him with me. Although he had no visible symptoms of leprosy, the disease could have been incubating inside him and so we quickly started him on the antibiotics.

He enjoyed talking to the two love birds hanging in a cage in my living room. We spent a great deal of time reading together and he learnt fast, proving himself more alert than I'd even guessed. He was always asking me what words meant. Back in Bababaghi he'd been known as a *bolbol*, which in Farsi is the name of a bird and is used to describe people who speak sweetly and a great deal. When we first arrived in Tehran though, he was quiet and observant.

Yet he did not seem unhappy. I thought he adapted remarkably easily to his new world. The fear he had at the beginning of our time together vanished over that first year and I even considered adopting his sister in order for him to have a real sense of family while growing up. He and I laughed together often and he developed a great sense of humour. He was confident talking to grown-ups and whenever my friends were around, Hossein felt included and engaged. He soon became completely integrated into my life. As a result, my mind was sometimes taken away from Kami.

The House is Black won a major international award in 1963, but garnered criticism in Iran. It was seen as an attack on Iranian society.

However, because of the publicity the film was receiving, the government was forced to step up its help for the community. Soon Bababaghi began receiving support from the government and the letters I consequently received from the community called me an angel.

The third edition of my first poetry collection was printed in late 1963, and that same year I got the main role in a production of Luigi Pirandello's play *Six Characters in Search of an Author*, an important piece announcing the arrival of modernism in Western theatre. This Persian production, a collaboration with the Italian Institute of Cultural Affairs and staged by a friend of mine, was a real hit in the capital. I played the role of the step daughter, an eighteen-year-old woman who has been a prostitute. It was my first theatrical performance and I was nervous about it, especially because some people from the company believed that I was given the role for being a famous poetess and that acting was not part of my repertoire. But I truly enjoyed it and expressing my voice through other characters.

In January 1963, Shah Mohammad Reza Pahlavi announced the 'White Revolution', a programme of reform that was supposed to be a step towards the modernisation of Iran. Many saw it as a threat to the traditional way of life, however, and in 1963 a cleric named Ruhollah Khomeini gave a speech in which he denounced the Shah as a 'wretched, miserable man'. Subsequently, an estimated 100,000 Khomeini supporters marched past the Shah's palace, chanting 'death to the dictator, death to the dictator! God save you, Khomeini! Death to the bloodthirsty enemy!' The Shah's regime was shocked by the public support displayed for Khomeini and two days later, in the early hours of the morning, Khomeini was arrested.

As the sun came up on June 5th, crowds of demonstrators came together in cities across Iran to protest against the arrest. In Tehran, demonstrators fought through government tanks and paratroopers to attack police stations and government buildings. In the village of Pishva, the Shah's soldiers fired machine guns into a crowd of villagers shouting 'Khomeini or death'.

Although I did not join the riots or demonstrations myself, I gave a small group of protesters a ride in my car when they were trying to get away from authorities. Even this small act of insubordination was enough to get arrested.

After spending hours at the police station being interrogated, I had to let them call Ebrahim to help me. It was the middle of the night and he was in the house he shared with his wife, so I knew how angry he would be.

He disliked being publicly involved with me but there was no other way to escape. As soon as I got in the car he started to give me a hard time. He thought it was a disgrace for a public figure like myself to throw caution to the wind and demonstrate with a group of students. He believed I was throwing my career away.

'It is not important what people think of me,' I said.

He called me naive and immature. He said that the regime was powerful, and reminded me that I was not immune to their rules.

Eventually we fell silent as he drove me home. He gently took my hand and begged me to be careful. Perhaps I am immature. Perhaps I don't want to grow up. Or perhaps I search for edgy situations that confirm my existence.

I tried to sign Hossein up for many different schools but each time I was told that he would only be admitted to the third grade, even though he was far beyond that level. One day we went for an interview and when the school director expressed doubts about Hossein's abilities, I took a newspaper off his desk and handed it to Hossein, asking him to read from it. Hossein was nervous but started to read beautifully. In Farsi most vowels are not written and therefore one must know the word before reading it. So when it came to the word 'Korea' he said the word '*kare*', which means 'butter' and Hossein fluently read us an article all about the war in butter, while we tried not to laugh.

E brahim and I developed strong, if unconventional, bonds with each other's families. I often spent time with Ebrahim's children, particularly his son Kaveh. Inside his family, my existence seemed to be handled with care and delicacy. I respected his children and felt close to them, and they also cared about me. I used to take Kaveh for drives in my blue open-top Alfa Romeo, with the wind in our hair.

The trouble wasn't within the family but came from the outside. It was outsiders who wanted to destroy the fragile balance we had all created together.

Hossein adored Ebrahim. The other day when the sun was shining in the sky, Hossein and I loaded up our Jeep with food and drink for a picnic. When Ebrahim arrived, Hossein jumped into the car and sat next to him with a big grin. Ebrahim immediately asked Hossein:

'Have you read the book I gave you? The *Tom Sawyer*?'

Hossein proudly answered that he had enjoyed it. His eyes were shining with joy.

'I will bring you another one next time,' Ebrahim smiled. 'Maybe *Huckleberry Finn*.'

That was a beautiful start to our picnic day.

In a letter to Hossein's father that week I wrote:

'Hossein is a happy child who is enjoying life at the moment.

He loves to play but is attentive in school and his teachers give him excellent reports. He is an avid reader and just finished *The Adventures of Tom Sawyer* by Mark Twain.'

I wrote to Hossein's father suggesting that we change Hossein's name and ID. When he was older I would tell him where he came from and give him the option to return, but for the moment I thought it better to keep things simple.

I wanted to give Hossein the best education and arm him with the tools to become a free-thinking individual who could cope with any tough times this judgemental society might throw at him in the future. I wanted to give him all the strength in the world, and all the confidence. I wanted to give him everything I was not allowed to give Kami.

Of course sometimes Hossein did stupid things, like any child. One time I even had to pick him up from the police station after he smashed a car window. Mostly though, he was an extremely empathetic and capable child who seemed wise far beyond his years. It made him sad to see me upset. When he accompanied me on a visit to my publisher recently, I thought he might cry when he saw me arguing about what I should be paid.

'You are bargaining with me for work that took me six years to complete,' I said to the publisher. I could see in Hossein's eyes that he felt my despair and saw how humiliating it was for me to discuss money in that way. He has seen me cry, scream, laugh, but he never appears to have trouble coping with it all. Perhaps

I let him see too much of myself, but I can never pretend around him. He understands the world.

Meanwhile, I knew little of Kami's life or personality, which was a great sadness. I wrote him letters but didn't know if he received them. I had no idea if he still remembered me, or if he ever expressed a desire to see me. I cried his name sometimes at night.

Today on a whim I asked Hossein to go and buy some poison for me.

I gave him the address and sent him off with some money. He looked perplexed but headed off confidently as if he were an adult. I tried to imagine what was going through his mind: what kind of poison does she want? Why is she sending me to buy poison?

It wasn't long before he returned, proudly holding a packet of cigarettes.

The social injustice under the Shah's rule hung like a dark cloud above us along with the rapid modernisation of Tehran and the increasing divide between rich and poor. It was a hollow society, progressing into modernity without having the foundations to accompany the leap. A desire for pleasure and wealth was taking over. People were losing their sense of identity and social responsibility. The freedom of expression that existed shortly between the forties and beginning of the fifties, until Mossaddegh's coup, was fading away with tremendous speed. To be a female intellectual was difficult in that climate of intolerance.

In April 1963, a group of intellectuals were arrested for plotting to kill the Shah, and given a death sentence. Around the same time the acclaimed Italian director, Bertolucci, came to Tehran to interview me and Ebrahim about our work and politics. We discussed how spirituality was draining from Iranian society. Bertolucci was interested in the nuances of being creative in a society where it was perilous to express any belief that went against the grain. This interview was one of the highlights of my career, because I felt that Bertolucci understood me.

Since no international reporters were allowed into the country at the time, Bertolucci smuggled out a letter to the international press about the intellectuals who were going to be killed without a trial. In the letter we asked readers to defend the rights of those who were not allowed to defend themselves, and it was printed in European newspapers. The Confederation of Students, with the help of Amnesty International and intellectuals such as Jean-Paul Sartre and Bertrand Russell, all united together in defence of those who had been arrested. The group of intellectuals were not executed in the end, but got life imprisonment. It was a dangerous time to be politically outspoken.

When I was young, I used to compose a few poems a day while taking a break from cooking or sewing.

Later on, writing poems expanded my understanding of the world and my emotions.

But now when I compose a poem, it is as if something is taken away from me.

A friend gave me a ring once. She said that it would protect me as long as it was on my hand, and so I wore it every day.

One day Pouran complimented me on it, and I spontaneously took it off my finger and gave it to her. As soon as I did so, I felt as if I'd done something unlucky and would pay a high price. It is silly to be superstitious, but I can't help it.

After Bertolucci's visit I was drawn to Italy again, so I participated in the Pesaro Film Festival and helped with a translation of Brecht's *Cercle de Craie* ('The Caucasian Chalk Circle'). While there I went to see a gypsy palm reader, a wrinkled old lady with a scarf wrapped tight around her head and tucked in under her chin. She had milky blue eyes and squinted at me as she told me I was in love with a man who would soon be involved in a terrible accident. I was so shocked at her words that for a moment I could hardly breathe and nearly fell off my chair. I was deeply shaken. When I got back to Iran, I told my sister that if anything happened to Ebrahim, I would end my life. My emotional life and my work were so intertwined that one only existed with the other. Ebrahim was my centre.

Ebrahim lives for his books. They are his faithful companions, his refuge, and his inspiration. They are his sincere advisors and sometimes I imagine that when he is alone with them he asks them questions as if they were people. His library is his sanctuary so today I knew where to find him when his family were out of the city.

For the last six days we hadn't spoken properly or seen each other intimately, just bumped into each other in the office. I was avoiding him because I knew we needed to have a serious but difficult discussion. I needed to tell him I was incapable of continuing as we were. Our relationship was at a standstill. I needed to tell him that despite all the love he gives me, I still feel abandoned. I needed to tell him that our love would die if we couldn't give it space to evolve.

Today I decided to be brave. When I entered the dark library room he was sitting with his back to the door, facing a window overlooking his garden. I could only see the back of his head above the brown leather armchair. The room smelled of cigarette and wood smoke blended together. It wasn't particularly cold but the fireplace was always lit when Ebrahim was in the library. When he turned around he seemed neither happy, surprised or sad to see me. It felt almost as if he had been expecting me.

With a neutral expression on his face he gently closed the book he was reading and asked me to sit next to him. I was feeling quite weak so I took a seat on the small rocker next to his armchair. I was ready to tell him everything that was in my heart and mind. I had prepared myself for this moment but suddenly, when face to face with him, it felt impossible to unpack my thoughts and emotions. I started my prepared monologue but it all came out sounding wrong and confused, while his voice was calm and soft. I wasn't sure if I was there to break off our relationship, or to ask him to prove his love for me.

Ebrahim knows me better than I know myself. His presence soothed my pains and slowly, while we sat next to each other facing the outside world, I calmed down. We had each other in both worlds. There was no reason to worry.

The fire was burning inside and outside us. It was the only sound I could hear. We sat there without saying a word. We were outside time. Our love was the source of life and creativity for both of us.

Yet now I am alone in my own bedroom again, trying to sleep, the clarity of our intimacy has evaporated. It seems I only believe in our love when we are together. Apart, it feels as if I am falling. My palms are sweating and yet I am cold. I cannot control my body or my mind. I do not want to be alive. I am not worthy of Ebrahim, or Hossein, or Kami, or Parviz, or my parents. I do not deserve to be on this earth.

I open my eyes and all I can see is white. The ceiling is white, the walls, the bed covers. There's a white plastic tube in my throat. Where has all the colour gone? Why are the colours hiding from me? What have I done to deserve this white cage? I can't remember.

White is supposed to be calming perhaps, but to me it is frightening. I need colour around me in order to feel alive. Instead I feel the threatening whiteness surrounding me, cramming itself down my dry throat. Colour is life and white is death. To leave the whiteness of the dawn each morning is to start to live. To stay in the whiteness is like refusing life. The only whiteness that I love is the whiteness of a blank sheet of paper.

Silence is also white. There is no noise around me.

I turn my head to the left where there is a medium-sized window with white light coming from it. In front of the window sits a person. It is Ebrahim. He is sitting silently by my bed, watching me.

'I know,' his eyes tell me. When I see him I want to live again and can't remember why I wanted to die. I want to be strong and survive. I imagine how perfect it would be if this silence could be broken by sudden music. I want to listen to Schubert, Vivaldi and Schumann. My soul needs uplifting.

I want to go outside and smell the little dusty alleyways of this city. I want to smell the earth. I need to be far away from this white disinfected cube.

I have done the wrong thing. Made a mistake. But I have never belonged to the group of people who believe they must always do the right thing. I become more creative through my mistakes. The world I live in is far from perfect, and neither am I. I will speak the truth until I have no more strength to write or talk.

There is no wall between us, there never has been and there never will be. Yet despite the joy that Ebrahim, and work, and Hossein have brought me, I feel lost. I am empty. I would like to go back to the beginning and start again.

I am disillusioned, personally and politically.

I always love the last poem I have written. Then I read it over, feel invaded with boredom, and itch to start a new one. I felt as if my youth had died, and with it my optimism and faith. A theme of meaninglessness is beginning to infiltrate my poems.

Sometimes I get confused when people try to define me as a feminist poet. I write about human beings: their beliefs, joys and pains, their desires and disappointments. My work belongs to anyone who is able to connect to it. Of course address the physical, emotional and spiritual lives of women, but women should not be the only people who can appreciate my words.

I will be fascinated by emotions until my last breath. And so I ask myself: 'Why do people want to die? What is it that brings them to the point of no return?'

The answer is simple: it is because of a lack of love.

Ebrahim's father was one of my favourite people. He was always open to new ideas and personalities, but most of all he was empathetic and understanding. He wanted to protect Ebrahim and my relationship in any way he could, and was even the one who spoke to Ebrahim's wife about why she needed to accept the situation, which she graciously did. Whenever I feel down and empty, I think of the warmth and kindness of Ebrahim's father.

It was thanks to his insistence that Ebrahim and I had a marriage ceremony, which meant so much to me even if it was not legally binding. I know that love has nothing to do with a certificate on a piece of paper, but I was thrilled to have an intimate ceremony that went some way to legitimising our love.

For me this ceremony was enough, and not enough. When I was feeling strong in life, I thought happily about the words of love and commitment we'd spoken to each other that day, but when the familiar nothingness began to fall heavily on my shoulders, I would think of our 'marriage' as a sham, a fake, a fraud.

I tried to ignore what people thought of me and to continue to express myself freely, but it is frightening to shrug off conventional morality. I have paid a high price for my decision to follow my heart.

Books, films, essays, acting, fame and interviews – my life is full and yet emptiness hovers. I will always be a lonely woman. I will always be a mistress.

The times Ebrahim and I spend together are beautiful, but also tormented. That was never going to change. He would never leave her. He was so outspoken about bourgeois mentality and yet part of him is conservative. Most nights, I sleep alone. The person who loves me is with another woman.

I visit my mother often. I do not see her as a role model, but she makes me feel safe and protected. She was a ray of sunshine in my childhood and although I know she disagreed with the free-spirited way I chose to live my life as an adult, she always tried to protect me from my father's negativity.

The other day she asked me: 'Why are you sad? You are an artist and you are beautiful.'

I answered: 'I don't want to be beautiful and I don't want to be an artist, I want to be happy.'

Monday the 14th of February 1968 is a beautiful winter day. I drive to my parents' house and my mother's face opens up when she sees me. She greets me with her usual smile and motherly embrace. I know she feels happy whenever I arrive to see her.

We sit by the window next to the terrace. In summer there are pots of herbs and flowers on the stairs leading to the garden but now the garden is totally bare. Even the pond is empty and the fish are dead. The only bit of green to be seen is on the pergola at the bottom of the garden, where jasmine leaves still grow in the cold. This year we haven't got much snow yet, even in the northern part of the city at the bottom of the mountains. This makes me a little sad, because I love snow.

Underneath the terrace there is a sort of warehouse, or *anbar* as we call it in Farsi, where we keep extra mattresses and tents for guests who stay overnight at the house. I used to climb on top of the mattresses and use them as a stage to perform opera arias.

The sight of the cold garden makes me shiver when we first sit down, but soon the warmth from the *corsi* oven underneath the table travels up from my legs to my whole body and envelops me like a warm blanket. But my lips are still cold.

'Can I have a look at your hand, mum?' I say. She smiles and puts her wrinkled, work-hardened hands on the table between us. I pick up her right hand and put my thumbs tenderly on her palms to look at the lines.

'This is your life line,' I say, tracing the line starting from the palm edge between her thumb and forefinger and ending near the base of her thumb. 'It's much longer than mine.'

'Would you stop this nonsense,' she says. 'Let's go have something to eat.'

We move to the kitchen to pick up the delicious lunch she has cooked: white basmati rice with a stew made of lamb, tomatoes and aubergines called Khoresh Bademjan. My favourite. The scent reminds me of my childhood. My hunger is for memories and I eat to remind myself of being a child. We bring the food to our spacious dining room, where our family of nine always used to eat together. It feels a bit empty today with just the two of us. I am in need of care and attention, perhaps more than ever before. I love watching my mother in the house because she always gives me a sense of security and protection. Her appearance seems unchanged through the years. She wears a cotton dress although it is winter, and over it she has a sort of working dress on. In the house she doesn't pay attention to the seasons.

We begin to eat and talk. Beyond the warmth I feel from being with her, surrounded by comforting smells and sights of home, I cannot ignore an eerie sensation of fear. Even though my body is warm and the food is wonderful, my lips remain cold.

'I've always thought I would die on a Monday,' I say to her as we are clearing away our plates. My mother turns around and looked at me nervously. It is Monday today.

Just as I am putting on my coat to leave, my father arrives at the house. My mother complains that it's impossible to know when he will show up, or how long he will want to stay for. As soon as he sees me he asks how Kami is doing.

'I have no idea how he is, Baba,' I say honestly.

'You see you didn't let me help you get custody and now you never see him,' my father snaps.

'One day he will understand everything and come back to me,' I say.

'It was stupid of you to let go of him. Look how miserable you are.'

'I am sorry but I have to go now, I'm running late.'

At the door, as I'm just about to leave, I have an uncommon urge to tell my father how much I have loved him and how much I have always wanted his approval. I had sadly failed to be a good daughter to him and I regret that failure deeply. I can't speak these words out loud though, so my eyes just fill with tears.

'I wish that you loved me,' I say to him instead. He stands speechless at the door as I turn away.

My mother walks after me in the cold, just wearing her summer dress.

'Did you come with your car?' she asks.

'I sold my car because I needed the money. I came in the office Jeep.'

'Comb your hair before you go,' she smiles. 'And please drive carefully.'

I turn towards her and repeat a phrase she loved to say:

'Whatever God wishes,' I say to her.

Epilogue

Forough drove from her parents' house to Ebrahim's studio, where she worked for a few hours before setting off home. On the way back to her house she tried to avoid a collision with a school bus and smashed into the side of the road. She lost consciousness at the wheel and died in hospital later that night.

Thousands of people attended her funeral on a cold winter day in the cemetery of Zahiroldoleh. Her coffin was carried through the streets followed by mourners. Everything covered with a blanket of snow.

Epilogue